In Silent Rush

This Fleeting Certainty

Angela Brownemiller

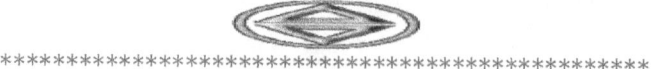

In Silent Rush

This Fleeting Certainty

KEYS TO
CONSCIOUSNESS AND
SURVIVAL SERIES
Volume 102

Angela Brownemiller

Metaterra® Publications

****

Metaterra® Publications
IN SILENT RUSH
This Fleeting Certainty
KEYS TO CONSCIOUSNESS AND SURVIVAL SERIES, Volume 102
Copyright © 2020 Angela Brownemiller.
Copyright © 202, 2012, 2013, 2014,
Metaterra® Publications.
All rights reserved.
All rights reserved in all formats and in all languages and dialects known or not known at this time.
Published in the United States by Metaterra® Publications.
www.Metaterra.com
Library of Congress Cataloging-in-Publication Data.
Brownemiller, Angela.
In Silent Rush/Angela Brownemiller –
1st Edition.
1. Poetry. 2. Brownemiller, Angela.
3. Browne-miller, Angela.
4. Consciousness. 5. Spirituality. 6. Ecology. 7. Politics.
8. Philosophy. 9. Theology. 10. Esoteric. 11. Psychology.
Title:
IN SILENT RUSH
Library of Congress Control Number: (see website listed above)
ISBN 13: 978-1-937951-14-6
Published in the United States of America for US and worldwide distribution.
Metaterra® Publications, USA.
Cover and content design & illustrations by and copyright ©Angela Brownemiller.
Cover photo credit, NASA.
Book design by and copyright ©Angela Brownemiller.
Ordering information and bulk ordering information available through: Amazon Paperback and Amazon Kindle and Amazon Audiobooks ACX.
also through website listed above.

****

****

****

****

Dedicated to

Earth

And its life forms

And its visitors
You know
Who you are

****

Table of Contents

Foreword:	
On Preventing a Poet-less World	11
1. Just Now Collapsing	15
Part One: Just This	19
2. So True It Hurts	21
3. Reigning	23
4. In Close	25
5. Seep Through	27
6. Or	29
7. Still the Waiting	31
8. Unfathomable	33
9. Faster Rush	35
10. Time Like	39
Part Two: Same Life	41
11. Not Far	43
12. Container	45
13. Same Side	47
14. Stage Wait	49
15. Of Course	53
16. Inaccessible	57
17. Shed Layers	61
18. Eonic	65
Part Three: Be Fooled	67
19. None Get	69

20. Catch and Release Me	71
21. Even Want to Say	73
22. Come Back	75
23. Higher Arch	77
24. Social Contract	79
25. Too	81
26. Pieces	83
<u>Part Four: Sheer</u>	<u>85</u>
27. No Whole	87
28. Faucets of Meaning	89
29. Sheer	91
30. For Truer	93
31. On	95
32. Cogent	97
33. Arrogant	99
34. Overtone	103
35. Limbo	105
<u>Part Five: Break Apart</u>	<u>107</u>
36. Peninsula	109
37. Weave	111
38. Alive	113
39. Believing	115
40. Right There	117
41. Bold	119
42. Simple	121

<u>Part Six: That After All</u>	<u>123</u>
43. After All	125
44. Unseen Self	127
45. Message	129
46. There I Saw	131
47. Nothing That Is	133
48. Spun From	135
49. Unwind	137
50. Moving	139
About The Author	141
Other Books by This Author	142
Metaterra® Publications	143

Foreword: On Preventing a Poet-Less World

Thank you for visiting these pages. I honor the poets who have preceded me, who have weathered centuries of time to remain in our hearts, souls, minds, and on our cave walls, parchments, bookshelves, and now in our techno, audio, and Ebook forms. And I bow to those poets of today who dare to walk these times where the poet is too frequently trivialized, at times all but forgotten, many poets simply left at the side of the road to fade.

We see how poetry is regarded as less than central, how the experience and the vision of the poet is too often treated as inconsequential. Yet what of life is not poetry? What of that ideal we call peace is not poetry? What of war is not best fought on the battlefields of metaphor, analogy, and simile? Where is wealth if not in the expressions humans can offer themselves, where they capture the moments they experience in the hearts of their phrases?

And what, pray tell, what of the human experience can derive itself from and represent itself in a poet-less world? Step forward now, human species, and protect what may be more endangered than we

know, that engendered species of life and mind, that life and thought form we call the poet and poetry.

Poetry has to stand up for itself as well. Poetry has to step forward and claim its power to express, in a way no other medium can, ideas that cannot be delivered elsewhere. Poetry has a complex multi-dimensional power it has yet to fully assume. Poetry can open new pathways in otherwise set minds-- even new neural pathways are possible. We poets must step up to the call, step up to our power, claim our place in these monumental times, in this parade of intellectual, psychological, political, spiritual, and artistic history.

In my work, I have seen the power of the emerging poet, and of poetry itself. I have witnessed this power during my years of working with clients and patients seeking refuge and healing in a harsh and for them sometimes virtually meaningless world where their creativity has been attacked, shut down, locked deep away for protection.

So many of these persons suffer from external and internal derision of the poets within themselves, the crashing assaults on their sensibility and pain that our modern reality fires on them. And I have seen so many come back to themselves through poetry, find themselves again on the road of healing expression.

I say let us make poetry entirely central in our lives, in our healing, in our training, in our education, even in our governing. Let us call the poets to the table, like philosopher kings, let us call upon the poets among and within us to hail and preserve this species of humanity we call ourselves.

        Thank you for listening with your heart,
                Dr. Angela Brownemiller

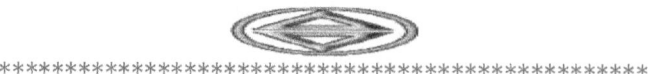

****

****

1.
Just Now Collapsing

In silent rush
The everlasting
Is dissolving

Just dissolving away

Like it all just changed its mind
Or was robbed
Of its core
Its truth

Polar caps
Collapsing
Revealing themselves
Their immense fragility

Now tenuous
Artifices
Of a nature

Whose message
We can only imagine
In our mind's eye

Whose cries for help
We can only ignore
So long

****

Givens
Betraying themselves

Now
Vulnerable intransigence
Apparent

But wait
Oh please
Wait

Stop
Stop now

Don't do this
Don't unsettle
This precious niche

We love it here
We think this is
Our home

Where we have
Lulled ourselves
Into dual indifference

Bold sense of
Entitled dominion
Over what is
Not really ours

****

****

But wait, stop
Please don't degrade
Not just yet

Don't dissolve
Away

Don't transform
This biosphere's status
Away from us

Not yet not now
We have only just begun
To understand living
Here

Still
In silent rush
With such fleeting certainty
We see the blaring scream
Of shifting givens

****

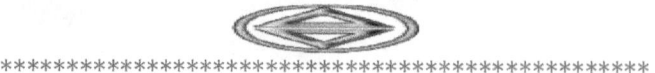
****

****

PART ONE
just this

****

****

2.
So True It Hurts

Such fabulous beasts
We humans are
Beasts of burden
Weight of our ignorance upon us

Our shoulders curling with struggle
Carrying this reality
This audaciously constructed reality
We hold so true

So true it hurts
So true it rings at the
Precipice of seeming wisdom

Where our words
Parallel each other
Their riveting mockeries
Conspiring to ease us
Into the shock of our
Startling nothingness-es

No don't spoil
What is so absolute
In the name of
The counterfeit
Calling itself sacred
So elementally false
Just one more rigid doctrine

And science no excuse
One more contrite paradigm
Poised to emulate significance
With its preciously narrow
Margin of error

3.
Reigning

Splaying outliars
Like outlaws
Like witches being
Burned at the stake
While their sins against reality
Reign still so victorious

Air fire
Water earth

Air
Air
Air
Oxygen

Poets' words
Subtle incantations
Invocations
Spoken into mist
Receding for safety
Camouflaging for protection

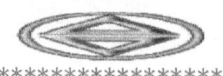

Lest the poetic license
Faces its revocation
Lest the license to exist
Be cancelled

In our rush
For meaning
In the still
Just this side of the other one

Where we dress
In all but nothing
To appease ourselves

To bully the
Looming void

4.
In Close

Get in close to these words
Swim these letters' little places
Dance between these seeming lines

Read the spaces in these sounds
The timing in these phrases
Where notes are written
And played on ideas

Now the tone of meaning
Disperses itself
Words singing like music
Until their own completion

Words like instruments once played
Now down at empty seats
Of orchestra members
Out for lunch
Eating lines

It is when
The orchestra leaves

The players go home
Their notes are stopped like words ending
Finished letters strewn about

The concert hall is empty
You can hear
The fierce crescendo
No silence so loud

5.
Seep Through

Seep through this window in time
You find yourself here in this room
Which is only here through this window
Only exists through this frame
Only is where there is also an only not

Nothing exists without a counterpart nothing
The opposite of nothing being

Stay tuned for truth to come to us
When we stand at the threshold

We are guests here
Our passports granted by that higher
Our passports to this place
Defined by the border of this reality

Who keeps this domain
Who protects these given boundaries
Who is this who
Who who
Unpack the who to find the non-who

****

That opposite of us determines us
By what logic we do not know
We wear this truth like reality wears us
Schizygystic donning of the robe

Our reality wears us on its sleeve
Which we determine exists therefore
We dress our reality this way
Bejeweled in glitter

Disguising us from
Ourselves

****

6.
Or

Ah, nihilism may be much needed relief
From the mandated dicta
We are so immersed in
Nihilism, or its welcome alternative, religion
Displaying brother science for dress up

Yet what is there without a higher power
Any higher power of ideas
Is it that this is higher
Or that this is power
Or that this is
Or that this
Or that
Or

We cannot know and should not know
What might extinguish the whole of us
Just by our knowing
Knowing

Knowing
Of this possibility that we actually do not exist

That we have not even dreamt all this
That none of this is here
Or anywhere

If you have the keys
Lock your door
Like your mind
For safekeeping
Believe nothing
If you believe you can live
Without a master paradigm
A higher power to respond to

A higher rationale to structure your thinking
To imprison you so safely within this reality

7.
Still the Waiting

Time waits
To unfurl its own diaspora
Scattering itself
Subjecting microseconds
To their own entropy

In this rushing still
Stays the waiting

Waiting
A presence in itself

While waiting
Moves in time
Yet waiting

Can stand time
Almost still

Nothing hurries
Like the still

****

The still then
Colluding with motion

To move
Nothing into something
Ethereal into material
Creating reality

More explicitly
More precisely
Than waiting
Tends
To do to itself

Time
Elevating itself
For all to see
To believe in

Time waits for no one
Not even itself

****

8.
Unfathomable

Transforming
Catalyzing
Idea into action
Notion into knowing
We are thus admitting
Truths into devolutions of themselves
Absolutes into less than certain to say the least

From unfathomable distances
Radiate hints
Of truth
Like footnotes to existence
Yes there is light out there
And in here if there is an in here

Proof of life
Or at least of light
Flicker
Flicker
Flicker
Radiating in from light years

Wafting in like time is nothing
Of consequence
Without the words to describe it
To note its passing
To say it exists

Where is time where there is
No awareness of time
Or does time know itself to exist
Possibly sentient
This lofty animal
Pervades us
Time is so fluid

Just as we cannot be fish in a sea without water
We cannot exist in a space without time
Nor can space perhaps
Unless it is born in the rush of the still

In the silent rush
Where the quiet never lapses
Extinction waits in the wings
Its clock ticking onward so patiently
Hesitating to trigger the great alarm

9.
Faster Rush

In the rush of the still
Racing waters
Wet with speed
Moving past themselves
Leaving their own waters behind

Dry wet
Racing
Rushing watery light
Enveloping time

Unwinding time from its
True cadence
Its own logic
Unfurling

Shaken
By truth

Denying time its structure
We find ourselves watching
While being watched

Bouncing lost in what
Was once called time

Now we the "they" are
The "they" that we are not yet or were before

Creation myths not withstanding
Test of time

Myth more persuasive than fact
More readily assimilated
More true

Where true is just what it says it is
True

Time revealed now for
The illusion that it is
Or was before we saw through time
Saw time for what it truly is

Or was
Or was never
Or was before we dared to question it

Which is not time moving
Not time passing
Not time in the traditional sense
Not time at all
Not time in any sense

Tic toc

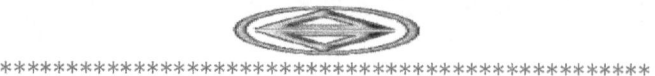

10.
Time Like

More time like water
Sweet water of reality
Seeping into illusion

Stilling the fire of false belief
The want of illusion
So hungry for truth

This thing we call truth
This truth we call true
This thing we call for
When we need our bearings
In this boundary-less universe

We can hang our hats
On the possibility
Even just the possibility of
Truth

This five letter word
Says it all

****

We grab it
Hug it
Make it our own
Truth truth

Truth, the given we have wanted so long
Is manufactured here in this
Underground lab
We call consciousness

The fool this mind who never lies

****

PART TWO
same life

****

****

11.
Not Far

We are not far from the time
When they will steal you
Or you's like you
For themselves
Wearing your face as their faces
Wearing your life as their lives
Wearing your memories as their own

Fear not that you are not unique
This wanton replication of your being
Will not harm you here
As you will not know
That this is taking place
Lest you read this warning label

Open this life with caution
Avoid sense of absolute identity
Stay away from self ownership
For your protection
Your safety

Just live knowing that all you are and do
Is being copied
For use somewhere else out there

This theft is nothing new
Just a duplication of beings
To lay out life elsewhere
This same life maybe
To write life
Already in progress
So no need to re-create

We are not far from the time
When they will steal you
As they already have:
Check your pockets

12.
Container

Like words
So inexact no true meaning
Washing themselves sublime
Though vague to the core
If there is a core
That is

Dissolving into
The blither we call creatura
For want of a better word
A better concept
A container of some sort
To hold ideas that can neither
Exist without perimeters
Nor parameters

Meaning without boundaries
Remains too very undefined
Meaning is not
As there is not
An is

****

This is is
Not
Or
Is it

The or
Itself
Is burdened
With indecision
Lost in this quiet storm
Of presumed intellectual decency

Eroding
Under the burden
Of worshipped reason

****

13.
Same Side

I work for the other side
Of what
Not sure as we all are on
The same side of this side of nothing
Or are we

They argue that they are real
The only real
They say

This they is what this is
This they is on the other side
I am they
We are they
They are they
Identity thus blurs itself
Into brighter focus
For a smattering of clarity

Best working it out at the
Synaptic level
Be the insurgency

****

Fight back
Detect their invasion
At synaptic firings see
Miniscule electronic deviance
Undetectable yet
Measurably appreciable

Aha heuristic analysis
Rivets minds with
No other options
Like knitting they sit
With their formulas and play

Play on the playground
Called proof
Swing sets of truth

****

14.
Stage Wait

Stage wait
Act one
Stand in for self
Don the robe
Face on
Wear the part
Wear you

Act two
Disguise to be that person
Slip into role behind
Façade of self
Is this the self
Or is self the outer layer
Or is mask itself the self

Act three
Yet all there is is self
In here
Inside here
In wearing the me
Shift in and out

****

In and out 'til the reverse is also true

Authenticity is relevant
On stage
Double bind the catch
Dramatic crescendo
Ultimate finale

But no curtain
Stage left you see you
Waiting to re-enter
Anchor yourself now encore
...
Afterward
Back stage
Disrobing

Ready for the street
Wash character pain from the face
From the looking glass

Looking back at self
Self emerging into mirror

Self surfaces
Or is the one who wore that paint

****

****

The stage face
The real self

And this disrobed one
Who played the stage self
From there behind the mask
Is this disrobed one now
No one

***

Stripped cold
Can I live
Up to this role

Can I truly play this part
Can I play me

No skill so sheer
No role so right
No robe so fitting

Yet to truly strip may
Leave me
Naked
Of my existence

****

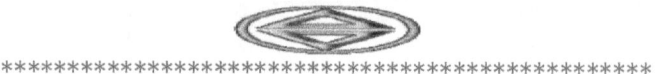

15.
Of Course

Suffer the truth
The lie of the looking glass

Reflection dishonestly poses
Insinuating that it is
Accurately reflecting what is out there

Yet reflection is not what is being reflected
Accuracy is sacrificed for presumed reality

Of course nothing we see
Is seen with much more accuracy
Than what the mirror reflects
And who are we if not mirrors

What do we see if not reflected
Shadows on our cave walls
Where shadows and reflections team
Imposters that they are

It is just that we have to see
That shadow of that reflection

Just to know that it is there
That anything is there

That reflection so double distorted
Made subjective by even the synapses
Not just the mind

Error is natural in the land of
The constantly inexact
Where of course
There can be no real honor in
Such mitigated perception

After all
When integrity goes
What is there

Some would say
If what we see are all lies
Then why look

Yet stay steady
Dare to reach beyond the looking glass
Where you find …

That other side
The side the glass has been allowing
Reflection to hide

Allowing presumed reality
To disguise the reality of the disguise

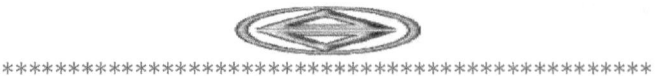

****

****

16.
Inaccessible

Who we are
Even that we exist is
But an artifact
A mere byproduct
Of existence itself

Realms out there
Inaccessible from here
In this form
In this mind set

Our paradigms will
Release us Tuesday
Or any other days where days
Appear to exist

This manufactured emotion
Is not felt but rather
Its feeling is programmed in

Ideals form nonsensically
Logic demeaning even itself

****

Irony in reverse
Hiding as reason

Unpacked
For all to see
What is not there
As substance is the issue

Material camouflage
A mask for nothing

Insubstantial substance
Hard copy of a mind set
Cannot capture itself
Within its own space

As all life leaves
For somewhere else
At some point

When this show is over
Or the parade is through

Blowing this pop stand
For another one

****

****

Like the mad hatter
As his tea party
Always rushing
To the next table

****

17.
Shed Layers

But I can't go there
Can't let myself
Shed layers
Break seals
Crack the code

Can't won't
Don't want to know
Yet

For
He who truly sees
Must truly see

Can this be known
Or selected out
To favor what is
Best not known

Yet do we feel
That tiny itch
Somewhere deep

****

Within our brains

Do we know
Do we care

Or was it planned that
We cannot know
As we are simply their
Bio-bots
Lab rats
Test runs

Bio chips implanted
Undetectably deep

We merely fleshing out
The mask for wiring so insidious
Its near perfectness
Resembles
Nothing less or more

So disassemble the resemblance
To anything
Previously known

****

****

We are not held responsible
For knowing
Up front or ever

No inquiry notice applies
Under such momentous pressure

Such ubiquitous duress
Of realizing we are trapped
By prior programming of our wills
Against our wills

****

18.
Eonic

Eonic distance
Between air and itself

Yet space so tangible
Distance so palpable

Findings so reconfigurable
Edges so indecipherable

Osmotic boundary factor belies itself
Porous borders dissolving

Eerily throbbing moving parts
Made of nothing

What is in there is out there

Collapse this down
Oversimplify to absurdity
So to not distinguish
And further blur for convenience
And safety

As knowing too much
Is risky for the knower

Foiling tell tale electrons
Spinning like truth in disguise

Truth masked
For all to see

Yet all see
Nothing more than they wish to

Nothing beyond
What they believe they see

PART THREE
be fooled

19.
None Get

Enemies of redistribution
Seek domination of realities
They define

None get all they want

Yet taking want apart
For what it is
Where want is need this is not want

Need never goes away
No matter who gets
There is always someone
Who does not

Want dissipates itself
Resurfacing as need great need

Is satisfying want truly satisfaction

We can be fooled
By satisfaction

****

When not shared is this genuine
Or simply hoarded satisfaction

Distortion of preference
Belies itself

Back burner
Simmering its distortions
Of want

Albeit solid it is fake
Albeit round it is sharp
Albeit reason it is merely
Mirroring images like fluids waving by

Illusions of gratification
Illusions of having
Illusions of an end to want

Illusions of never needing again

Those distributing know the games they play

Casting want and need together in the same pool
Of their own distortions

****

20.
Catch and Release Me

Fish for it
Fish for the one dropping babies
While being reeled in
Tiny fish falling out

So now you have caught me
You will release me
Caught and released am I free

The lie of catch and release
Release from what
With what

Harm as a souvenir
Do no harm is a joke
When harm is mostly all there is

Catch and release yourself from yourself
And see how this feels
You say better than being caught and kept
Kept for what mind you

****

Eyes watching their killers

They say to us
Don't say this
We do not want to know what we do
Do we

Do we go there
No not really
Why ask or beg such a question

Just release the wonder
Just let go of the doubt
Just close your mind and walk away

Leave the fish behind
Best not caught in the first place

What is it we are catching anyway
Unless you are a hunter
Seeking gratification
Wielding keys to this
Prison you feel you own

****

21.
Even Want to Say

Those bothersome
Infinitesimal immensities
Nothing like a universe to startle a cosmos

Parallel times equaling
Duplicate moments seeping by
Times washing away
Hours evaporating
Into black holes to recycle
Waiting to be reborn as new moments

Collapsing histories
A colossal waste
Diminishing the significance of time itself
One might say were one to even want to say
Which one is not

Neither here nor there are really consequential
Nothing much makes a difference
Not even the beholder

Yet the eye of the beholder

Can read into what it sees all it wishes to see
And this is substantially valuable
In the reality game

Ah yet reality is merely a game
Believe it or not is all there is
Give it all you have or give it less
Or give it nothing
Ultimately makes less than any difference

A little like when in the room
The women come and go talking
Just talking
Reality is just a seven letter word
Important is just an illusion

22.
Come Back

Come back to the reality game
Pay your money take your chances on
On
On
On what
On chance itself

It is the chance you are taking
Not relevant on what
Chance is just the thing to
Keep us going on this gamble game
We call

Life
Life
Life
Spin it

Chancing it is all we do
It all is chance
Each step
Each breath

Each each

Chance is in everything
Chance of showers
Chance of rain
Chance of no rain
Chance of chance

23.
Higher Arch

Lest metaphor for all this fails us
We can run to the temple of high worship
The bank
Where we see the higher arch
Of this hierarchy
Or at least its signs
Barely visible to the eye

Yet the imprint is sensed
An invisible hand is there
Pressing us
To bow to the
Mega corporate mega national
Inter world

Even after the fall when power disassembles
Temporarily revealing itself for what it is
A glimpse in view
We discover this power
Is immovable unshakeable still

Surrounded by our

Forest of knaves
Shadowing themselves
Their beguiling dominance upon us
We feel their stupid belittling
Merely imposed for its own sake
To beckon us into compliant idiocy

24.
Social Contract

Social contract
Mimics a higher agreement
Baser levels of ourselves
Agree to appear
To be less base together

Social contract not to
Social contract to
Social contract to contract
Social to social
Or not

Come to the floor you notions
Admit that
It is either in the word social
Or in the word contract
That the pseudodoxical truth
Reveals its nature

Nothing to take for granted
Except that taking for granted
Can always be done

****

Whether or not reality based

Which is again that game
Of believing just to
Believe
As an act of
Confirmation
To still the
Looming void

And again
And again
And again
Trudging obediently
On and on
Locking in the blinders
Just to see through this

If you can get out
Run away
Run away now
Safe distance:
GO

****

25.
Too

Bottle this nihilism and market it
It beats the actual void
Or masks the engulfing
Gulf
Between what is and what is not
Something to hang onto in a pinch
Precious invalidation

Savor this emotion
Into oblivion

Walk away just
Walk away from
This
Concept
Too true to be valid
Too obvious to be actual
Too plain to be simple
Too too to be too

26.
Pieces

You who are so ubiquitous
Pieces of me are yours
Where there is a me

Pieces of who I could have been are also yours
As I somehow gave these to you
Or you took these as your own
When I could not see the difference

What is left of what is me I have to salvage
Earnestly assembling a self
Fragments of me are finally mine

Jigsaw puzzle pieces assembling
Out of shattered stuff
New picture of self is formed

***

When you feel this
Cherish this
Feed this

****

Protect this behind closed doors

Just don't alert anyone
You are finally here

Predators seeking a self
May again track you

****

PART FOUR
sheer

27.
No Whole

With purloined status
Like a self proclaimed god
Your chosen diatribe
Raking me over the coals

For what purpose exactly
What reason vaguely
Can you disassemble reality
Into these components

For us you say for us
As we are great together
We form the universe
This is our reality

Still no whole is truly greater
Than the sum of its parts
When the actual synergy of the
Parts themselves is admitted
To entirely rely on
These parts themselves

****

Components are never
Merely components
They simply present the
Illusion of being parts of a whole
Greater than themselves

A whole we will never detect to make claim to
As the whole whole is more
Infinite than anything less than itself
And resides in each of its parts

Each part of the whole already so whole
A hologram of itself within itself

Like a shifting mirror
Forming an ever-morphing
Reflective mobius
From which there is
No true escape

****

28.
Faucets of Meaning

Waiting like seconds
Dripping from faucets of meaning
Time pours
Itself out of its container

From where does it flow
This thing we call time
Writing itself into
This dimension

For some reason
Unintelligible to we meek
Vaguely thinking wizards
Taking a
Mental ribbing
For knowing too much of

Nothing

29.
Sheer

Sheer micro filaments
Invisible threads of being
Intertwining

Love wildly weaving a tangle
Just to establish one's existence
And another's presence

A surge of demand for validation
In a sea of in's
In- in- in-
In sufficiency
In adequate
In auspicious
In valid
All so in opportune
In
In
IN
IN
Or out

****

Some kind of quasi string sort of
Theory
Superfluous on its disappearing
Secretly entangled
Mobius surface

Take that first look last
Look at it
Peer through this
Eye hole

Into a sea of
Compassion
Washing over
And around
And in

Duplicitous empathy awaits
Like fool's gold
All who enter these doors
Will be caught but not released

****

30.
For Truer

For truer
Convolution of the
Straight up
Disguised as erect
For want of a better term

Just inside the outer layer runs
A filmy substrate of self
Its contour radically ill defined
Juxtaposing angels
Insinuating lost triads in space

For want of a better concept
To hang our hats on here
When in actuality
Nothing this is
Is ill defined
Once defined

It is the definition itself
That wants
Our ideas

Flickering into sentences

Specious algorithms
Casting themselves as valid
Applying the tool of words
To establish presumed legitimacy

We can wear this lie
It fits us
As we fade to next scene

31.
On

On off on off on off
On on on dot on on dot
Dot on dot off
Dot dot dot
On and off

Binary is never binary
Yet neater to think of than tri-nary
Or multi-nary or infinite-nary

So do it
Think it
Go with it
For the basic sake of
Sake itself

Bit bit bit
Eat tasty bits
Gourmet information modules

Chips abound now
Dipped in electronic juices

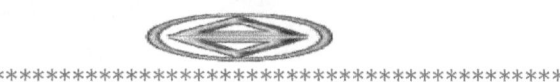

****

Savor the disc
Where your life is stored
Like a library of you
Reduced to
on offs on offs on on on

Best not to power down
Too soon
Battery life not included

****

32.
Cogent

Meeting of the minds
Like palms rubbing together

Their cells breaking off to join
Some unknown nether world

Falling into the ether
Blowing off like ideas
Flagging in the gusts of analogy

Wobbling like
Weakening backstories
Failing to withstand history

Their gravity winding down
Centripetal consequences
Falling off

Parading as
Reverse sequels to each other

Such a cogent diatribe
Unlike the ranting
Logic of nature

See its rabidly alternate nature
Just match the meaning
To the source

But please no cohesive display
Of understanding
No illumination now

Try not to infect this panorama

33.
Arrogant

Beat the pervasive yet tacit nebulous
Dressing itself as anything but
Sloppy thinking
Presenting itself as a set of
More than proven hypotheses
As foundation for this structure
We dare to call reality

Fight this

Yet if we wish to strike out
With the sharp arm of clarity
A weapon powered by its
Absurdly arrogant certainty yet
Such a precious resource in a world
Where actual clarity is scarce
And bullshit masquerades as fact

They will run from the
Shock of the distinctly verifiable
That can even purify the tainted
Arms, tentacles

****

Invasive probabilities of
What we are told is true

Take it in carefully
Really breathing this in

Then gasp as
Reality shock
Stings with truth
Its fragments hitting and piercing
Bubbles we think are our worlds

So welcome to reality
Take a gamble and step in
There is little risk

You face merely hairline odds of
Actually dying here
Chances are slim

Dying in the face of
That clarity greater than
That which truth says itself to be

But a moot point

****

****

Coming to terms with this
Equivocation can mean
Florid displays of pain

****

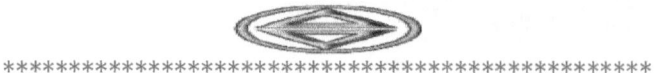

34.
Overtone

We meet
Glimpses of who we are
Reflecting deep within each other's eyes

No immediacy better than this first look
No now more lasting
Than this moment
With its absolutely pure instant
So rapidly passing

Yet with such
Grand immensity
So infinitesimal
Albeit the key
Tuning fork of the universe

Overtone reverberates within all the
Sequential cosmoses beyond
And yet this is just us

Two souls passing in the night
Hungry for this second away

****

Never to know each other like this again

Yet to carry with us this
Singular moment of peace
Amidst ongoing wars on all levels

This island in time
This illusion we call
Peace
This thing we want
Peace
This action we take
Peace

This state of mind we have fabricated
To believe it is here
Or somewhere to be had

****

35.
Limbo

Time you are so silent
I know this ticking of your clock
Is only a game
Merely a mask you wear
To parade as something less alive
Just a passing commodity in space

These tinny ticks of your clock
Say what though
Time where is your actual voice
Bellowing out from
So deep within your recesses
Where your heart itself beats time

Please just shout your P.O.L.
Your proof of life
Time you are alive
A life form who does haunt me

Time I know you must see me
I feel your eyes upon me
I sense your stalking

****

Please confirm yourself
Your sentience
Just once startle me with your cry
So I know you know I know you know
Startle me
Please just
Startle me

Here in limbo
I found your note
You said wait until time gets back
Out for a drive on a sunny after cosmic noon
But waiting for Godot could be easier
My intransient friend

I don't like you

****

PART FIVE
break apart

36.
Peninsula

Fish to find it
To break apart the knowing
To see there is only nothing
Through the looking glass

Be there for it nevertheless

Peninsula of substance in this space
This lie is manufacturing itself
To be consumed as truth

A future Trojan horse
The nature of which we will only know
Far too many millennia later

Millennia in the counterpart universe
Where we are already marshaled
Into this war zone

Inducted to fight this force's battle
For what
To what end

Why

We somehow are not told
What this battle is about
We somehow do not see
The battleground on which we stand

Yet there we are
Running point
For a higher order
Where we are pawns

37.
Weave

Weave this streaming light
Pulling strands
Filaments
Threads glistening

Intertwine these soft beams
On this loom of space
Warp and weft
Tapestry of energies

Pulsing carpet woven
Alive
Magic carpet ride

Vast iotas
Gleaming spindles
Sheer threads

Single fibers
Micro light
Nothing yet ever imagined

Rivers of essences
Flowing like water made of nothing

Fine invisible strings
Washing into the flow

Creating the gloriously pure
Glisteningly sheer
Every day penultimate
Moment

Before infinity

38.
Alive

Light is alive
In itself a sentient
Life form
Its intelligence
Parading so inconspicuously
Before us
Its original existence
Being foundation

Yet still further out
Beyond all boundaries
Where there is not even light
There is indeed
An "is"
Isn't there
As an "is not"
Is an "is"
As well

When you finally fully accept
This "is" as parody of reality not reality
Do not quiver

****

Stay stable for all to see
Order pizza
To calm your neighbors
And grant them their stupors
As they grant you your own

As no one stupor supersedes another
Yours however is your own
As is your choice to wake up alive
Somewhere beyond this drither

What a world this would be
Were we all to get it at the same time
Could that many break free all at once
Or would the balance be so upset
The higher ups could not take it

***

Now when you are ready
Remove the mask
They can't stop you

****

39.
Believing

Believing is an art
Not heralded as such
Yet entire civilizations build from
This substratic practice

Believing
Winding its way into daily lives
Ancient and modern

Shhh!

Speak with decorum
This is a grand epiphany
An efficacious aspect of ourselves

We support this consensual delusion
Just because
We march under orders
from a high imprint

Shall we pray to this master
This intelligent design

Or have we fallen prey
To these intelligent designers
Who wrap our fates deep within
Their coding of us
Their program code in double helix

Evolutionary genetics
Such spectacular camouflage for
What is really going on

Invest
Invest
Invest in knowing
Investigate what
You are not allowed to investigate

Know that who you are
You are not allowed to know you are

Believing takes on new meaning
Itself a mask for such pervasive mesmerisms
The ego we have manufactured
The greatest disguise

40.
Right There

Right there
Between the air and itself
Between what is between and the between itself
Between nothing and all that is not

In no space there is space
The illusion is good enough
When we
Do not know the difference
Anyway

Split hairs for finer
Units of analysis

The myth of the measure
The truth of the false parameter
The ism of the an-ism
Trades under the table
Like a secret dealer

Pristine and rather cellulosic
Crystals of precision

****

Needles of time
Spiraling in like
Sharp darts
Piercing the skin of now

****

41.
Bold

Auspicious
Audacity
Trying to hum tunes
Like vibrations of spheres
Totaling more than sums
Of their parts

Total infinite
Ultimately infinite
Time for wisdom has passed
Wisdom an artifact
Of perception
An artificial algorithm for valuing

Yet value declines as value defines
As it is pulling into presumed
Clarity the vague

Know this value is so purposefully vague
To protect the truth
Shield it in protective obfuscation

Delay the great unveiling
Avoid the moral hazard
That walks far too close to really knowing

42.
Simple

Simple clarity does not lie
Or does it
As truth wears many shades

In fact the more you look
The less you see

The more you believe
The less you see clearly

The more you argue your point
The less you sway even yourself
If you are really listening that is

Yet who will listen to us
Who can really hear

Yes we elect
So called representatives
To represent us

Yet clearly no one can fully speak for us

Not for each of our thoughts and tendencies
And wishes and beliefs
As these manifest moment to moment

Even in a democracy
People change their minds a lot
Sometimes unbeknownst even to themselves
Let alone to their representatives

What a folly to assume that even we
Can represent ourselves

PART SIX
that after all

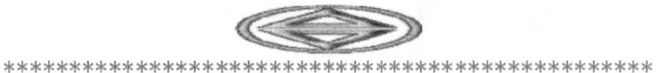

43.
After All

Waiting on brain cells to get
The obvious
And assimilate it into meaning
Again

Synapses themselves lagging

Our knowing itself
Simply a belief system
A shot in the dark

A bolt sent into the
Electronic petri dish
We call the synapse

You hide yourself
Yet you don't know who you are
Or who you are hiding from

Who is this self you obscure
For safety
For sanity

****

For remaining so under cover
Simply fighting for a credible reality
For some reason

We are calming into this stupor
This lovely acquiescence
Or so they think

Yet we have them fooled we believe
At least they can't touch us we say
If we their lab rats
Can believe in our SELVES
That we do exist

We must try to not know this
Not rationally
Or we will be detected
Well perhaps only arguably rationally
Even rather perspicaciously

Safety
Take the notion to the table
Find it frozen in wrestle pose
Down at the mat
Hide your true consciousness

****

44.
Unseen Self

Immediacy
Penultimate instant
Riding unseen waves of space
Like dark horses
Secret beams of eons
Racing into real time
After waiting in the wings
For eternities and more

You ask
Is this a friendly vacuum

Yes
Nice to meet you here

You see
I have been you before
Oh yes you are me
And so am I

We are here together
Meeting for the first time ever

Yet spawning each other from the start
Ah this mystery of the nil

Do not wave at the fellow traveler
He is a salient nihilist
Like you unlike you
And your
Pedantic agonistics

All the same either way
As you are that person too

Don't be concerned
You will not harm you
Any more than we have

45.
Message

Message in a bottle
Written long ago into the future
Sent back to be
Read in advance of finding it

Easy to do
Just think about it

Believe it and it is there
Open the lid

Recover the message
Already writing itself before being written
Already speaking itself before being said
Already about itself before being about it

When there is nothing more to say
There is always this
Disaggregating truth

Unraveling itself
Into pedantic versus

Dogmatic versus
Fanatic
Depictions of truth

Busting through the confines
Of an insidiously pervasive norm

Stay here at this
Log jam where the
Eye of the needle splits open

Freeing the angels once trapped
Dancing on the head of that pin

46.
There I Saw

It was there I saw
Several bolts of
Jagged lighting
Strike repeatedly
A jungle forest tree
Beating open
Its tarantula nest
So many giant ones
Escaping and racing
Up and down the tree
A sight to see

The laughing children there
Put the giant ones on leashes
Like pets those playmates
While other tarantulas
Flew the jungle forests
With their
Six foot wing spans
Over the land

****

Where back in that old hotel
The old man played his
Laughing box
Over and over
For the woman who
Shattered every mirror she saw

When the shamans of yesteryear came to see
They robed themselves in now
To make an appearance
In the eyes of a plastic god
No longer there either

****

47.
Nothing That Is

Subtle wafts made of unseen
Invisible moments
Flowing to compose time into
Nothing that it is
And all that it can be

No substance
But then what is substance really

Reality sucks
But then so does nonexistence
At least from this perspective

We have to exist to
Contemplate not existing, right?

Suffer this fools' delusion
Nothing like this
Port of fathomed realness in this
Storm of depleted belief

Or shall we just smile and walk away

****

Just smile and move on to the next picture show
Ok let's blow this pop stand
Been there done that got this t-shirt
Having worn this life
Worn it so proudly like a won justice

But not even the jaws of this divine court
Could bite truth from
The tongue of its own lies
Justice weighing in
On itself

Heavy handed gavel pounding
Slamming rulings
Against themselves
Depleting honor
From the process

L-shifting into same place from another angle
Just to be there

****

48.
Spun From

Specious dreamings
Deceptively compelling
Connected like spindle tissue
Spun from steel fields of hay
Built out of
Art-like containers
Cells for nuclei not gelled into life yet

Coacervating
And waiting
For eventual evolution
The most intelligent of all designs

Selection is natural
We are led to believe by this design
Which includes the design of
Our belief mechanism itself

The brilliantly intelligent
Design of our evolution
The absolute best lab test

****

Species exist as beta test functions
Ultimately working in reverse

Pre manifestation particles
Propel into the nasty stasis
Of pre existence
Numb
Dull
Pre vacuum events

Alterior motives originate
In alterior species of thought

Where the biosphere is merely
Made of races of
Linked synapses

Neural communities
Nothing more

****

49.
Unwind

Charged now
Hyper reformulation
Crystal fractals alive
Transcend themselves
Shatter into conscious particles

Smaller than fractions
Sub chromosomic
Sub sub chromosomic

Fracturing even basic Fibonacci
Schema they impose upon themselves
Marking stochastic spasms

Like catastrophe theory
A wave until it breaks of its own force
Showering itself
Power too much to bear
Foiling its own purity
Unwinding its own expression
Into the still

****

Again in this still
Stays waiting
Wanting time
To unfurl its next diaspora
Cyclically

Again scattering itself
Subjecting ever sacred
Micro milli seconds
Diminishing fractals of themselves
To their own perpetual entropy

Yet all this proceeds much more explicitly
Than waiting tends to do to itself

When again we find that in our haste
Nothing hurries so much as
This relentless forceful
Tumultuous still

****

50.
Moving

Here
The silence
Races

In this rush
Of the still

Where
Nothing thunders
Like broken stars

Their racing sounds
Moving like
Crashing water

In the moment
Of inception

The rush itself
Isolated
In time before time

****

First
Comes into being

Born
In that loud loud rush of the
Wailing screaming still

Listen you can hear it
Feel it in your bones
Touch it with your spirit

And then you know
You finally know
You are really here

****

****

About the Author

Author, speaker, journalist, psychotherapist, philosopher, human consciousness researcher, poet, Dr. Angela Brownemiller, also known as Dr. Angela®, is author of over seventy books of nonfiction, fiction, poetry, and genres between or beyond these. Among her numerous collections are the books in her *KEYS TO CONSCIOUSNESS AND SURVIVAL SERIES*. See DrAngela.com and Amazon.com for more information and additional booklist.

Author Contact:
DrAngela@DrAngela.com

****

****

OTHER BOOKS BY THIS AUTHOR

Among the Books by this Author,
Dr. Angela Brownemiller,
are other volumes in this ...

**KEYS TO
CONSCIOUSNESS AND SURVIVAL SERIES:**

Poetry and Consciousness:
Volume 101: **THROUGH CRYSTALLINE PRISMS**
Volume 102: **IN SILENT RUSH**

Consciousness, Survival, and Psychology:
Volume 3: **UNVEILING THE HIDDEN INSTINCT**
Volume 4: **HOW TO DIE AND SURVIVE**
Volume 5: **OVERRIDING THE EXTINCTION
SCENARIO**
Volume 8: **NAVIGATING LIFE'S STUFF**

See also these books by this author:

SEEING THE HIDDEN FACE OF ADDICTION

THE POLITICS OF PERCEPTION

Additional works by this author are listed on:

Amazon.com
and
DrAngela.com

****

****

Metaterra® Publications

Readers, walk with us,
share in the harvest of
culture and mind,
spirit and soul,
idea and letter,
history and the time it travels….

Metaterra® Publications seeks to bring together modern and ancient issues and ideas.

Metaterra® seeks to harvest the matrix of intellects and wisdoms, to develop new and build on existing and old approaches and philosophies.

On the Metaterra® book list, you will find both nonfiction and fiction, and some of what lies between, and some of what lies outside these parameters. Consider this Metaterra® Central here and beyond.

www.Metaterra.com

****

www.ingramcontent.com/pod-product-compliance
Lightning Source LLC
Chambersburg PA
CBHW071225090426
42736CB00014B/2976